Sight-
ings

Sight-
ings

Patrick Friesen

Winnipeg, Manitoba
2026

CMU
PRESS

CMU Press
Canadian Mennonite University
500 Shaftesbury Blvd.
Winnipeg MB R3P2N2
www.cmupress.ca

CMU Press is learning and striving to create an inclusive and welcoming space for people of many identities and communities. We work on land which is the ancestral home of the Anishinaabe, Cree, Dakota peoples, and home of the Red River Métis. We are grateful for their stewardship of this place.

Editors: Eve Joseph, Nathan Dueck
Copyeditor: Sue Sorensen
Designer: Marijke Friesen
Printed in Canada by Friesens, Altona, Manitoba.
ISBN 978-1-987986-29-7

Library and Archives Canada Cataloguing in Publication
Title: Sightings / Patrick Friesen.
Other titles: Sightings (Compilation)
Names: Friesen, Patrick, 1946- author.
Identifiers: Canadiana 20250276119 | ISBN 9781987986297 (softcover)
Subjects: LCGFT: Poetry.
Classification: LCC PS8561.R496 S598 2026 | DDC C811/.54—dc23

For my love, Eve

Contents

Maps

Some things that happened for the first time
seem to be happening again
—"Where or When," Rodgers & Hart

or speak

I hear you singing
at night your shadow moves
along the wall

the sound of ancient hooves
outside the window

how did you get in?

it's the song
I heard at the river

who are you?

you touch my hand
and whisper over
my shoulder
I can hardly listen

or speak

the human voice
empty and
waiting to be filled

each night is the last night
the song coming to an end
everything coming to an end

well, not everything

Out of the Past

attending

the noise of relentless contact
with the world, that nightmare
of data without the tenderness of
silence, or whispers, *Pay Attention!*
the klaxons of belief,

nowhere is timeless, deep in the
interstellar travel of dreams there are
whimpers and cries, our lonely
mad species navigating through sense
and thought,

the intimacy of falling in love with
sweet nothings on a wind phone,

or a fox crossing a field in its wild
loping presence, an invisible
songbird waking trees at sunrise,

some desert traveler said nothing
is written, in sea or sand,
he was wandering on foot and
in mind, longing, he said, to be
the one at the oars.

lies and beauty

1.

it's been a long year of brutality and
shameful words, a greed for carnage,
for extinction

have we arrived at a time
when a car horn in the night
brings terror?

do we remember each person
beneath the bombs, each person
we did not meet?

2.

how often the world has been
obliterated, with each death
it vanishes

cinderella with her slipper, the
shifting tide, the stars, *the magic
flute* from a green radio, all of it

and litters are carried, the wheels
of hearses roll, and the world
falls away, rehearsals are over.

3.

the weather has turned fatal and
I have not wasted time enough,
not taken in enough earthlight

but there was a day when
I heard someone whistling,
and I caught a childish glimpse

that was before I fell into words,
before lies and beauty and the possible
difference between them.

heron-minded

heron-minded and standing
inside the patience of desire,
the navigation that happens,
ears of stone listening to our
motion, want happening like
the slow grinding of glaciers,
and stories move from the sea
to dry land, hungering into song,
the beauty that lessens fear,

dreaming sea shells and kelp,
ankle-deep and wading between
striated stone and tidal pool,
life and more life, womb-
stunned beings that we are,
all worship and distraction,
afloat in coffins of ancient
cedar and cobbled brass,
but still we dream the dream
of origin after origin,

the bones of hundreds of
thousands of years, who
did they belong to? all
those burials from before
us, the rituals, who were
they? disappearances
from trees and caves, lost
moments, like the sudden

strike through its reflection,
the raised head, and a fish
sliding down the gullet into
an ancient hunger.

(Found #2)

...............blind
..............o deaf

...............cochlea

............sparrows
..............and

...............audition

...............snail
.................etina

....
............and the rain

creature

from beneath montbretia leaves she emerges,
slow and brown and lies in the dirt, abandoned
in the heat, curling her tail around herself, dying,
she looks up at us with something like wonder, an
intimacy that shreds the membrane between us
for a moment, perhaps like lawrence and that
sicilian snake, and she's oblivious to our hands,
to water and seeds, closing her eyes, done

with seeing earth, oblivious now to the sun and
warm soil, flesh sinking into the soil, known for
a moment, unknown, perishing into words, how
the dying leave, already elsewhere, already strange,
but still smelling earth, and opening eyes once more
to see the familiar guests in their perfect forms.

blossoms

magnolia blossoms at five o'clock,
flowing in the wind, and the
dark blown water holding
the metaphysics of a lonely child,

living in the memory of memory,
somewhere between absence and
extinction, which is a presence if
your feet are firmly on the ground,

and you, alive within the questions
and relentless thinking, alive within
the sweet and savoury, alive with
what your species fathoms,

the limits of beauty, of what you
hear and taste, the drawing in of
breath, this is what you know, and
yellow poppies along the path.

returning

you have a corner of garden
with montbretia and prairie grass

there are days you tell time
by the gardens in your life

or perhaps by the dog who slept
in a hollow among the tulips

while you are on earth
it is difficult to believe in absence

what you remember is a door
through which you entered

some arriving horizon
a place to set yourself

what you have is a chair
beside japanese irises

or there's no chair at all
could be

(Found #7)

.....................................an old
woman.................................
..............................and two girls skip
............................boys taunting each other
.......................beneath a jerusalem tree,
.............................burned out with sun,
aching....................................
....there
..........................only the weird sound of
inconsolable laughter.

darkness of matter

the body beautiful is eternal as long as
the ghost lives, and who has not seen
a beautiful body, and who cannot love,
who cannot reach for the other? longing
for the unfamiliar, that hand, that mouth,
alive in the bewilderment of matter,
finding a way to love mortality.

mulling the darkness of matter, like
orgasm at 3 a.m., bodies beneath
a white duvet, as if they were buried
in snow, the brilliant white snow of
the moon, and them all flesh and hair
and nails and losing themselves in
the soil of each other, seeded in the
darkness, in the depths of death, a
rapture and a separation, and then
a hand reaching for the lamp.

bog man

the mirror is wearing gravity's mask,
it was always there, invisible, but slowly
through decades fastened itself to your face,
and with the doubt it holds there is also
a restless ecstasy, this moment of time and
carrying it to an end, a bog man in some kind
of infinity, a flare of astonishment among
the tactics of survival, a tuna sandwich,
a job, all the dysfunctions of the species,
and the greatest of inventions, love,

and underground a cello is grinding
its lowest note, the machinery of earth,
your feet feel the vibration as you find your
way on a fool's journey, walking sometimes
through the alphabet of trees, or drawing
the hanged man from a pack and
someone banging sticks together, or
palms on river water, the percussive heart

and the release of something hidden, an
elation of dance with breath gone raspy,
and then a cry, how can one live without drums,
the clap of hands, a return to the earth,
and falling into the arms of a name, oh
the moon is a cold stiletto blade that entered
the womb and cut you free.

bones, again

bones fusing, the boy shaping
into manhood, his cranium
knitting like his grandfather's,
like the annihilated sapien, even
radius and femur gone, he raises
his arms to the morning sun, from
mandible to phalanges, he lives
hand to mouth, crouching in
long grass or clambering a tree,
cawing like a crow, becoming
words, and bones, again.

corpus

corpus, that's a truth, the body laid out,
the whole of it, prepared with perfumes,
or ready for the furnace, the work of it,
what it held, hands that moved in air
like words, long feet that walked through
many cities, the whole body, the flaw
become consummate, a corpse as it always
was in the beginning as at the end, mother
labour, delivery, sparks from a bonfire into
the night, star-battered and all our questions
returning.

hidden face

the rubble, the masonry of theology, and
beneath it a river, abundant dark and loamy,
a wound of the womb, a first birth before
the mirror, and you are not a heretic for
there is nothing to be heretical about, you
are here and there, kissing and holding the
other, the face before you, the unfamiliarity
of it and the strangeness inside you, that
hidden face with the erratic conversation
that goes nowhere, the flawed wonder of
such intimacy, and the startle of laughter.

(Found #11)

..........................you don't exist, she said,
....though it was
a little vague......................................
................................and it turned out she was
....she was talking
too much light lately................................
....burning like a torch,
....
....beneath a street
light,

whispers

whispers in the house, heard yes, but
forgotten until later by the child, so much
history in those whispers, moments
that slid away into a swamp of forgetting,
sinking among the reeds into dreams,

he remembers a whisper, his fingers still
on the piano keys, a whisper from his
father to his mother, he doesn't remember
the story, but he remembers his father's
shadow through the door, a man who
never whispered,

and then, hearing liszt on the radio,
a phrase returns to him, though it
was there all along, rising now from
the marsh, and then a sentence, and
it comes together, the song, words,
something about tears and a dying woman,
and he turns to the radio, to that familiar
melody,

he recognizes who the woman was,
the grief held back in his father's murmur,
this is how stories arrive, how they vanish.

a gust of wind: 1918

was that the first intimation? the flower garden wilting,
and hollyhocks leaning away from the house with no
one to tie them back, no birdsong but for the rooster
at dawn, and a distant bell from a nearby town,

a child at the creek, sitting barefoot, head in hands,
listening to the water's silence, then raising his head
and turning toward a coughing fit from an open window,
a grey cat drifting like smoke along the foundation,

and the sun rising and lolling across the sky,
uneventful and metrical, and always in the brevity
we are, but on this dying day, this child's last day,
with a sudden gust of wind he is orphaned.

whistling

a sound not much heard anymore,
a tune, yes, but a sound, a breath,
a man walking to work in the early
morning, whistling as if each inhalation
is a gift to be returned,

in some small town, or the bronx,
someone whistling on the street,
or an alley in toronto, wayfinding
with pursed lips, that breath departing
into the world, was it the 50s?

an oriole in the garden, or
a house finch on a post, the kind
of morning a child never forgets,
absorbing the melodies and lives
of these bright singers,

and the day has no name, it's
just the absence of time, a promise
being slowly broken, and *slow*
is time, a killdeer running circles
with a broken wing,

and the man returning from work,
me roosted in a tree, the man passing
beneath, whistling an old hymn, a kind
of reassurance, the song of a worn man
released on a breath.

hangman's drop

hangman's drop, the knot, and sudden fall
through history, enough, I am tired of nations,
tired of lies, I could be many men, a drunkard
with grog-blossoms on his nose, a cleric with
his briefcase, I could be my father, or someone
who resembles him, I could be a ghost trying to be born.

no saints, no angels, no more excuses,
it is enough to sit at a rough table with a piccolo rum,
watching fishermen launch their boats,
this could be manarola, it could be here,
I move up and down the stairs, between mind and foot,
all this disappears in a few years.

there is something unexplained about a rope frayed to a thread,
a thread which cannot hold the weight of a great edifice,
the weight of thought, only the hem of a moment, a woman, let's
say, sweeping broken glass out the door, that is enough.

the future, again

1.

was it a lone tree or standing
small in an orchard? birdsong and
sun through leaves and dappled
shade, a quiet moment on earth
when an apple loosens, detaches, and
plummets, drawing heaven to ground,
all that holiness brought down,
the apple rolling through grass into
sunlight, a bruise about to turn brown,
and decaying petals fluttering on
the path.

2.

a chanteuse is singing about
the distance between stars
where romance begins and
where it ends, all those horses,
knights in their armour dying
in strange lands, the crusade
story fraying, diviners calling
for the prophecies of a falling
star and losing their way on foot.

3.

and us with our harvests and
children, walking fields and
crossing bridges, falling to our
knees in peril, coughing in bare
rooms of anxiety.

us refugees praying to walk
water, raising our hands to
a great silence.

the ghosts of gods in chains, fear,
broken rituals and the words we think
we need as a scaffolding of certainty.

4.

the door closed and open in the same
moment, while everything changed,
and me standing there, about to leave,
and leaving.

5.

and another bairn born.

welcome little animal
catching your breath and
carrying death with you
from the womb, the joy of
you on earth, a stranger
becoming known.

and wouldn't you know,
someone remembers
the future, again,

and the apple keeps rolling
away (it seems).

(Found #19)

...........................cold universal space,
....................................in a long arc
....of its birth,
......................................for a moment,
a hummingbird....................................
....earth's dancer,
....his brother's
....snow
....footprints
....around the fire
...........across the frozen lake.

peonies

them blowsy peonies don't know if
they're good-looking or dying, spread
out like a rosy funeral dress, and the
amnesia of the streets, invisible
bodies walking by, turning toward
the scent of peonies, overwhelmed
and sorrowed, and the senseless
living oblivious of the parfumerie,
smelling only the dead they cannot
see, amongst them.

desertion

mother's fingers at the piano,
perhaps *wiegenlied*, the spirit of
sleep, your consciousness thickening,
that last moment of clarity then
beguiled into a desertion like no
other on earth, and the music has
betrayed you and vanished, your life
sinking deeper than night, an odyssey
without harbours, losing your life to
a dream, your hand slack on the pillow
beside your face.

questionable evidence

a green thought, a red one, quicksilver thinking, course
changes abrupt, connecting, disconnecting, sideways,
parallel, and no words to deliver any of it, me without
a shakespearean vocabulary, far from it, that facility
to bend, appropriate, ultimately to translate, the weird
work of associations, trying to slow them down, trying
to shift them into some kind of order without damage,

simply unable, sitting in the green shade, getting up to
walk my way into language, trying to find a way to say
it new again, the same old, but vivid today, all that motion,
the chemistry of it, and nothing comes together

though I hear the static of the radio on a passing tug,
see a man at the wheel, and the water, as usual,
the water seeps into me, but I can't fathom it, ideas
flowing out of some hidden folds of the brain, unconnected,
unworked, lost, that particular collision and commingling
irretrievable, and the thinking disappears, as does the man,
and the few laboured words that come, these words leaving
only questionable evidence.

this ghost house

what we have ...
dead ancestors and the weather ...
each of us on the way ...

our brief sojourn ...

longship voyages ... it may be ...
rivers ...

sparks from train wheels ...
and deserts with their hunger ...

a stop in time ...

a moment ... another day without a name ...

coffee and a danish ... say ...
or the naming of a birth ...

an ancient man on the beach
laughing at memory ...

at some story ... and him
losing the words ...

the thunder of artillery ...
always ...
and plunder ...

or desolation ...

and stories erased ... leaving
striations

on glacial stone ...
a scar fading on an old hand ...

and us singing
our children to sleep
in the ruins of this ghost house ...

look

look, the lacey beauty of worm-eaten oak
leaves, your heart holding at almost 80, the grave
digger leaning on his shovel, and shostakovich
coming through someone's window, pretending
to be jazz, though god bless the 5th, an orange
cat stalking mice in the swale, and you're holding
mail in your hand, straight into the recycle, the
door is unlocked, your love asleep upstairs, and
there's not much more you want that hasn't
already passed.

incarnation, eating spirit

incarnation, eating spirit, eating myth, eating
at the table of fallen gods, us eating memory,
and beginning again, in light and earth, wading
across the river, shucking off *enjel und alles
heilich*, holy pickerel gliding through water,
sheltering beneath a willow's overhang,
shallow breaths, air bulbs, gobs of gossip, and
me just born slippery, sliding through every
mother's hands, reptilian and fishy, landed,
dazzled, and looking for a reason.

contradiction, a horse of a different colour

contradiction, a horse of a different colour,
going the other way just to be going the other
way, meeting an agreement and turning away
to find a side road, a dirt road, with knee-high
grass between the tracks, slipping along a
foot path at an angle to the river, rolling up
pant-legs and wading upstream to douse
my scent, sins glowing like an aura and me
turning again, heading back, nodding at
the fox, a blackbird falling from the sky, or
is it rising from the marsh?

disputes

damned by crescent and cross,
deranged by circles and triangles,
well, why not, there's enough time,
there's enough room in the asylum,
there's enough world for an asylum.

and you forget all the damage,
you drift from some inner life,
from anything important and
you know the relief of drifting away
and you don't care, why would you care?

there is a small chapel inside you
that you've been rehabilitating,
doors blown open and wind rushing
through until there's no room, until
there's no certainty, no fable.

too easy, there is an addiction
to overcome, and the new one
to massage away, though anger
remains waiting in the open grave,
a freeing breeze off the sea.

there is no relief in the world,
though you walk in the rain, you
know patriotism is a dead word
along with prosperity gospel, all
that swagger and shame, how sad.

but in here, with the chapel in ruins,
a radio rouses waves of ecstasy,
and fear has to become courage,
the inside disputes can be raucous,
can be soft, you listen closely.

insisting on a way from home, away
from codes and passwords, slapping
lousy hands that reach, evil hands
in the posture of prayer, or theatrical
gesticulations of dominance.

your hands are chasing a fly ball,
it's shape and motion, it's hunger
and sensuality, it's death, and it's not
godliness, the next thing to godliness,
good god, godliness is godless.

interstice

you have broken away and come to nothing,
a place in which to inter seeds, a dark
soil in the night, beneath a full moon,
where quiet upheavals begin, and fear
finally drifts away, there are no werewolves
here, only the dream of a howl that
wakened you long ago out of a world
you couldn't leave and into a world you had
to enter, living in the interstice, where
the monuments have fallen and the
defining stories are out of breath, where
emptiness is possible.

(Found #20)

...................................yourself,
.....................................the story
....there,
....a wonder,
....and
....................................a yarn you have
....though you
....unraveled,
....like
all them animals.....................................
this is your word..................................
................................receding.

laughter

only to say I was seventeen, in a pew,
suddenly aware of absurdity, fables
in the face of the cosmos, and I fell
into laughter upon laughter, waves
that couldn't stop their momentum,
hand uncovering my mouth to release
a wildness, like irrepressible music,
a radiant wedding of mind and lungs.

it was breath, the body's desire
to be that fearless moment, a snort,
and people turning to stare, then
laughter rising to the ceiling, breaking
into streets and town, heard, it is said,
at thirteen-mile corner.

which is to say there was no holding back,
and no pleas, no anthems, no letters to sign.

the body loves absurdity, standing
in an open doorway, no heaven
on earth, nor anywhere else, just
the planet and us a stray species
slipping on a banana peel.

and it returns, when needed,
a blessed turbulence in the face
of certitude, and I trust it will
visit at death, even if silent,
my mind breaching.

road

I was walking on the road to where
I'd never get to, stopping off in granada
to lay my worn-out shoes at the root
of the dead tree, though it wasn't
a dark night that day, it would be
arriving before I knew, though I knew
it was coming, the place where
all tales end,

was it the language my mother taught
that sent me away from her? the road
that opened up because of the words
I learned, or my translation of that
ballad she sang, the music of her voice,
my turns and swivels, break and entry
into moon work,

not much to say, the journey becoming
archival, the folds of my brain closing
over, hiding the stories we all were,
me still telling them as if for the first
time, a father a mother, a pack of boys
yelping in trees without names, growing
into funerals,

us boys standing roadside, caps off
for the slow hearse, and imagining the
body behind the small curtain, inside
the coffin, remembering hands and mouth,

the blessed body returning home to
nowhere, my eyes blinded for a second
by the sun off silver chrome, that's how
any day goes, reflections and shadows,
yes?

reflections

the shadow of a tug in the mirrored
lights of the city, that engine throb
guiding the bulk of a barge, its
shouting workers, the distant calls
of silhouettes that come through
as if rising from the dark water of
some hidden world when the moon
was cold and unremembered, before
stories were told, let's say a still winter's
night and someone shouting on the
shoreline, the shape of a memory
still clinging to a circuit in our primal
brains, a flickering scene, a fire and
that sapiens call across the water.

the engine pulse of the tug fades,
and you see what's apparent, another
city, a reflected city, a sinking city,
its lights descending slowly, leaving
behind flotsam, small machines and
music, almost audible, the tools of
builders, and you see dead men and
women at café tables, with their rings
and watches, and you hear children
laughing as they listen to olden fables,
as they fall asleep and disappear slowly
into the depths, water glittering for
a moment like gold leaf, then dark.

harbour road

us being old and hand-in-hand walking
down harbour road, and it feels as if my
hand is her hand, how they meld, and
the crows and gulls above the water
are poets, the gulls crapping everywhere,
crows sleek as parsons, and they speak
untranslatably, filling the world with
ancient sounds, and her hand is mine
for a brief and infinite while, the water
tousled by a breeze, and an uneasiness
in the clouds.

an old woman in an old man's arms

from anti-matter to this, at dawn
blinds brightening, the sun finding
its way between the slats and shaping
a chandelier sliding slowly along
the wall, the sun finding an old woman
in an old man's arms, their fingers
entwined, fingers that have touched
so much in this material world,
two old people who almost don't
matter, talking their way awake
and laughing in that moment of
human devising, love, alive and
living toward

impasse, no words

a table lit by a light, a table with an empty book,
and a chair worn to a sheen, bare feet beneath it,
a light at night, a light that keeps the corner
dark, a corner where the secret of the room abides,
some fetal shambles at the rim of light, that
moment of birth and death, and the clicking of
a keyboard, well no, that's not it, there is no
table or keyboard, and there is no book, only
an unoccupied chair and a dark corner, let's say
nothing else.

the other side of the window

gazing out the second-floor window
at the harbour, losing words which the
waters remember, vocabulary in the deep,
the swimmer of the first water now rowing
toward a final wordlessness, an ecstatic
recognition, a crow gargling in the magnolia,
a heron on stilts, and me no longer sleep-walking,
finding myself on the other side of the window,
stepping into the mind of water.

(Found #21)

a thousand waters flowing..........................
..............................who can know them all?
....the sound of a silent
room...
turning a page..................................
of shifting earth...
....the memory
....drenched
....in *symphony*
....can hold so much
sound so quietly...
is not silent at all...
....where the music lives?
....in the water
....of the water stairs,
....sliding over
stones..
....long after
my only life...

river time

river passes by and wind
which ruffles the waters

call it fish street call it motion
the fisherman casting for his reflection

born like a belly flop in time
the river opens for the child

swallowing matter like saturn
eating his only-begotten son

and the river flows past the mouths
of caves where humans worship

on the bank animals slaughtered for
ritual spill their blood into the river

the drowned sink and disappear
hands waving as they go under

the water whispers of origins
memory drifting downstream

and the river closes once more
leaving the river within the river

rivers

Maps

Squid

He sits on the edge of the tub, brushing his teeth as he has done thousands of times before. He hears a tsunami in the distance. The room is unfamiliar for a moment. As is he. Sentences grow shorter with time. He tries to lengthen them, one comma at a time, pulling conjunctions out of the air. Can a squid be thirty feet long? There are stories of tentacles holding a ship, and there are stories of ancestors in frozen sleds. But, you can never use *but* at the beginning of a sentence. Says who?

Map

He woke, lying there like a map. Rivers and streets and hills. A body, he thought, a body that had nothing to do with him. A calendar. Thursday, perhaps, or the quiet of Sunday. A machine, rusting in disrepair. Yes, a frayed old map. The capitals of all the provinces. A slap if you didn't remember each one. The colours at the back of the Book, Canaan, the route of Exodus. An urgent voice once again, and boredom. Bicycle paths between buildings and the highway into the world. Trying to leap over Monday and land on Wednesday. Or, later. How old do you get to be?

Sightings

There is anguish in light. I'm drunk, she said, having never touched a drop. How else would you explain this broken mind? But she remembered an eclipse of the sun. 1863. No, July, 1963. That was when her first-born disappeared. Deer are difficult to spot when they're lying in tall brown grass. They're good at not being where they are. You wait. And you wait. Until an ear twitches. Trains used to whistle. There was that. Feels like a floatplane, she said, trying to rise from the water. You leave things behind, sorrow for one. There were sightings, she said, there were sightings.

The Trick

Disappearances and appearances may be the magician's fundamental trick. I watched it happen in my garden. He made a card disappear, though a moment later a gust of wind blew it from his sleeve. There were other disturbances. Wild laughter, for instance. And an old man, sitting on a threshold, said we couldn't see him. I remembered the child in a tree who said no one could see him, his hands covering his eyes. And it was true, I couldn't see the old man, only the queen of spades in his invisible palm.

Silver Hearse

I'm waiting for the ferry behind a silver hearse. The woman driving it wears a white shirt buttoned to her throat. There's a hawk gazing at us from the top of a light standard, and I'm not sure what this movie is called. Sometimes conjunctions are dream words connecting scenes. Sometimes dreams are movies you stay to watch again and again. On the other side of the water the hearse speeds past me, and then I pass it. The driver looks crazed. It's not Emily Dickinson. We keep passing each other. Suddenly the sun catches a corner of the burnished casket, just a flash of light through the gossamer curtains. Redtail hawks are known as opportunistic generalists.

A Free Man

You can't catch Leviathan with a hook. You just row your boat quietly into a bay and wait as Leviathan dreams you. You have caught perch and, once, a walleye, and you have written letters to the world. *And and and.* This is a dream word you live with. But you have never tried to catch a whale with a worm. You are an old man now, walking naked through the house, talking to yourself like a gurgling baby in its crib. Leviathan sounding. You will die a free man, your hands raw with rowing.

Not That Far

He heard Spanish at the foot of the stairs. Other languages too. Flemish perhaps, and one of the Slavic languages. A slight movement of lips, when words are intended but don't quite come, can mean yes. Or, it can be an acknowledgement. A movement that lives between things and expressions, partaking of both. He heard Coast Salish about halfway up, and Japanese a few steps further. He was just guessing at these languages. It's all about sound, not meaning. He had read that somewhere. And it's not that far from foot to head, the mind moving between the two. There was wordless singing at the top step, and whistling. He heard footsteps. They weren't his.

Species Dance

You were laughing, and I was abandoned to absurdity. We sang for a moment on the steps, the night around us. I slowly learned that I am something less than a poppy, a montbretia, whatever. I am passing myself on the street, stopping now and then to watch the species dance. Finding out the song doesn't matter, only the sound. Like a guffaw.

I Want to Return

I want to return, if you don't mind. It's not the blood on the stairs. It could have been an open wound on a foot. It's none of the above, or none of the below. Leave that to the birds and fishes. Pause. If only there was a god, the story could have a beginning. Pause. And an end. Someone is singing, always singing. It goes on. Can't get a word in. But, what would that be? Just for a moment in Neolithic times. Stoned. But, that's not it. It's academic, an academic nosebleed. It's the wild horse at the river.

Ghosts Don't Sing

Some pray with hands placed together like a steeple. Others interlace their fingers in a closed clench. Ghosts don't pray, they appear. And ghosts don't sing, that is for the living. A way of measuring distance. On earth, as it is on earth. Music holds immense vocabularies, vibrations of the universe it has been said. Like the tremor of hands that have lost their way, a sign of time. It's a comic opera with too much story, and a fool finds his way to the sea.

Unbelievable Stories

Wading in the water, shoes in hand, I'm watching a distant freighter fade into the horizon. What do I know of trails in the sea, or the pull of magnetic forces? My friend Paul believes you can't understand Greek philosophy until you've stood under the blue Greek sky. There is another theory that Greek philosophy began in harbours. Certainly some think sailors tell the most unbelievable stories. It's never about the journey; it's always the end with them. Eschatological, a theologian might say. Buffleheads disappear and surface, disappear and surface. Returning from the underwater music.

A Cello in a Rose Garden

Cello music in a rose garden might be impossible to focus on, distracted by the scent and colour of roses. Of course, if the rose garden is too geometrical, and too cultivated, that would be another distraction, more unfortunate than the others. Some say music is mathematics, but a mathematics that bears little relation to the architecture of pruned trees and bushes, or to the sculpted lawns. The dead lie beneath the roots, trying to sing, though because of distance can no longer sing in close harmony. But with good ears one can hear harmonies, sometimes the dead a few feet apart, sometimes hard snow miles away beneath a full moon. Each knows their song, their cry for the world, breaking a silence that remains unbroken. In his room a young pianist is practicing scales, a sound that leaks out across the night-time cemetery, where the only other sound is the sighing of trees.

The Bell Across Five Miles of Fields

He could hear the bell across five miles of fields. It was not part of his world, but still he stopped to listen. Wondering how long it had taken that faint reverberation to reach his ears, and was the bell silent at that moment. He was a child, a boy who was baffled by silence. It seemed to be a memory of some other place. How did sound emerge from silence? His cat often surprised him. He'd look up from reading, or he'd turn his head, and the cat was there, standing in the doorway as if it had always been there. And, he thought, it might have been. Who could say? The metallic taste of water from the garden hose being the taste of the bell just before it was struck, at the rim of silence. That's what occurred to him, without thinking, one summer afternoon.

Fugue

He wakes not knowing where he is. The last reverberations of a bell tells him he is not at home. He doesn't mind. Raising himself to a sitting position he sees a cathedral tower in the distance. People are milling about in the street a few floors below him, selling things it seems. Hovels everywhere. You need poverty, he thinks, to create wealth. But, still, they have the church. It is something he recognizes from his world. If he dresses, goes out into the street, and just walks, perhaps he'll remember where home is. Or, if the phone rings. Yes, someone from home. Still naked, he sits in the chair beside the telephone. Music drifts in from another room. Bach. A Bach fugue, he thinks. This is how it begins.

Maria Brodsky

There is too much light sometimes; it gets hard to see. Too much heaven too. All those people levitating in elevators. I was eating a tuna sandwich, sitting on a bench with the name Maria Brodsky on a brass plaque. There was more, the dates of her birth and death which told me she had lived into her 90s. *Love is the last privilege*, it said. I tore the crust from my sandwich and threw it at two crows waddling nearby. Yes, too much heaven, of everything related to heaven. Too much setting sun in my eyes. And the sudden thrashing wings of crows, their silhouettes, multiplying like miracles around Maria Brodsky.

Normal

There is no normal in normal. That's what the graffiti said. The man lay in the hospital bed thinking of escape. A passenger train rumbled by, shaking the room. That relentless motion of imprisonment. Pretending to be going somewhere. Someone in a church pew, bent over in prayer. Always the fear of derailment. Heaven's above, cried a nurse entering the room. Get back in bed, or we'll have to strap you down. Birdsong first thing in the morning, so loud and joyful coming out of a dream, can shatter the day into fragments. There are no tears on the cheeks of the weeping preacher, his ankle fastened to a star. But then, that's been said before.

Essential Tremors

The old are vulnerable. Flightless birds too, when there are rats about. My neighbor is a musician; each evening I hear her playing slow glissandos on her clarinet. Sounding like glass about to break, sending shivers up my arms. It's evolution they say, birds that lack a keel bone. His feathers floating on the sea, Icarus was brought ashore and buried. That's the story I heard. *A boy falling out of the sky*. And a ship sailing on to Byzantium. Or Ithaca. Some silent place no one gets to.

Crossing

The one at the oars always has his back to the future. He rows through reeds and late shadows as his passenger stares at him, or rather over his shoulder. There is an idiocy to philosophy, to all that star-gazing. It may, however, help guide you, traveling by heaven, to some hidden harbour from which you'll never emerge. That would be Thracian laughter you hear from the trees. The passenger doesn't even smile; he knows what's arriving. Oaken oars creak in their oar locks. There is a splash in the dark, like a dolphin diving.

Unraveling

In his old age, the man spent hours in the back yard unraveling stories he had grown up with. His grandfather's story of a death on the tracks. His mother telling his silent father's stories. Weaving is a difficult art. The Bayeux Tapestry embroidered the story of the Norman Conquest. Arachne angered Athena because she wove brilliantly and said she was greater than the goddess herself. Athena destroyed Arachne's weaving and transformed her into a spider. The old man took apart story after story until he found his own. The story was yes and no, woven loosely, with a flaw. Unraveling.

Boxcars

Is there such a thing as hope within a dream? Dreams are shunted about like boxcars, though there's never been an empty dream, has there? In the 30s hobos dreamed food and shelter and work. They woke up for hope. Boxcars have been filled with many things, including nightmares. I know a man who learned to pray in a boxcar. He wanted to stop motion, and he seemed to succeed for a while, his feet on the ground, though he understood as he was dying that he hadn't succeeded at all. Truth stands still, but only if you dream it. You can hear boxcar couplings rasp as the train slows to a stop.

Unforgiving

A ski trail ends abruptly mid-field beneath a white prairie moon. Once upon a time there was a man in the moon. A forgotten yarn. Everything disappears, even myths. An owl sweeps the snow with its heavy wings, leaving a drop of blood behind. There are many stories of winter, though most of them sound unbelievable. They're too cold and unforgiving. Men lost in blizzards, women dying in childbirth in a snowdrift. And there is the story of rapture, but then, that's theology, isn't it?

Lonely As

Is there anything as lonely as an empty playground? Or, a laced-up shoe in the ditch? Sometimes you can hear the underground conversations of trees. Villages, towns and cities. Or, gulls gathering above the water, wheeling about and talking. Someone once said that we are made human by words. That is one of innumerable beliefs I don't hold to. The cry of a rabbit in the talons of an owl. A moment later a snowy moonlit field.

Like Goya's Dog

A simple sentence says what you need. No more complexity coming apart in a sentence diagram. Still, there is the intricate universe when you look up like Goya's dog from the mire, feeling the non-entity you are, with just a slight breath from your corroding lungs. What do you make of it? That expiration, and then inhaling the next, finding it helplessly. Hands trembling and an agitated wind all night. What can you make of the orgasm beyond comprehension, a gasp of nothingness, the abyss of formation and collapse? Like parsing *Finnegan's Wake* into a river running through the mind. Finding shape in Babel for a moment. A simple street in the rain, the scent of arrival. You don't understand that beauty until it's necessary.

Homages

joe: remembering joe rosenblatt

slipped into the bridal stream, the fishy brides
he dreamed gliding among the reeds

joe working long ago for uncle nathan on the
blood-gobbed sawdust floor, clubbing the living
ghost out of a pickerel, all slimy parts, gills and
heart, that violence

and the betrayals of family, mother and the
bearded ones waving him away from the table,
the tired rebbe with his drink and venerable smile

and night came, and the waters were dark where
he learned to cast his line, him walking on ruined
feet through feral fields of serpent bird and muse,
bard of the fantastic, the shadow of a dragonfly
hovering over him, briefly, then gone

and now he is unmarrowed and untentacled and,
yes, he has slipped away to marry the alluring brides.

butoh

hijikata, twisting his body, gazes up to the balcony where mishima has begun his ritual, what he has believed his way into, a last room, hijikata with bruised legs and gestures, his hands dancing the darkness of the dead, an intricate anatomy, vessel and muscle, the body becoming ash, alive and distressed, the shape of a broken soul, and mishima, worshipper of the body, mishima, the sailor, sailing toward nothing, a vanity of mind, all that courage, while ohno dances death into old age, his body thin as parchment, a grimacing damsel.

among the leaves of light

like someone shattered, so wide open
no one can enter, nagle holds the stage
without thought or intention, her bag
filled with masks and icons that do her
no good anymore, a walking broken
heart, sorrow says the script but she
passed that on the way to the theatre,
downstage now, exposed by the gobo
in the gate, all burning focus as if she
could go up in flames, then it shifts,
and she escapes among the leaves of light
on the floor, motionless, standing like a
tree, and a cello supple as it descends
to the bottom of sound, playing dark
through her fragility, a willow, perhaps,
that bends but won't break.

koestler's window

it's what we're all born to koestler's window a spanish courtyard
and the unredeemed mathematics of death
a telephone ringing at the end of the hall with its lonely alphabet
waiting to come together as a sentence
and history doesn't matter nor prophecy only the window with its
flagrant and insufferable possibilities

you wake from what you can't possibly remember from before your
birth from that awful ungodly slumber
of wars that go on and on a kind of species *selbstmord* with all that
righteousness and anguish
or waking back into the deepest sleep of rivers and all you've
forgotten carried in that current

the window is open staring in at your rumpled sheets and gazing
out at the stain of mountains
the telephone dangles black and stiff from the wall a garbled voice
ranting amongst the dying footfalls
beneath your sill a dog circles the soil of its sleep settling with a sigh
among the closed red tulips

circus

walking to the circus, deft steps and hoping
to find a story, something like that movie,
pina bausch at the *café müller*, watching
and guiding all that blindness and ransack,
banging into the wall of love, a cigarette
between her fingers, or miss ophelia flaw
going through her positions of worship
in some lateral world, on her knees and
rising and knees again, my brief story a narrative
of the childish question why, maybe the man
on stilts with his face in the clouds, or
the tumbling acrobat seeing earth and sky
flashing by, yes, maybe that, the somersaulting
clown with his weeping eyes, and I'm born
into the past, not knowing if it's past at all,
water sliding over stones, over my bare feet,
rain coming down long after my only life

desert

walking into desert, harry dean walked away from loneliness
and, like rilke, into solitude, a baseball cap shielding the thousand
lives of his face, the man looked for his wife but found only
story, which he left behind, like an extinct language, or wearing
cargo pants and an oversized double-breasted jacket, stood
in front of a smiling mariachi band, locating, in his ninetieth year,
the depth of his voice in a song of childhood and grief, the desert
had been waiting for him like the emptiness of a hearse, as it
once waited for rilke, heavy-lidded with rose petals, yes, they faced
the desert, gazing until they were blind, and walked into it.

blood oranges

always a black dress in the closet, and
a bowl of blood oranges on the counter,
there is a symmetry joseph builds, with
deliberation, out of the clutter of words,
aware that something may be hurtling
toward her like a seraphic train blowing
through the station, eve of lost ancestors,
indomitable, even in the grievous house
of her father's dying, in a room of no
rituals, only the gesture of her hand on
his reconciled hands, a daughter's birth-
right, a moment of familiarity at last,
leaving the house to walk along a dirt road,
stopping at a field for the horses at the
fence, their ears tilted toward her sorrow.

ghost in the lintel

she calls the spirits with her sisiutl crossbeam,
nicholson shapes human hands and a face
between the two heads of the serpent, calls
for their welcome, for the open door of the night,
and on earth there are passages, there are
roads of renunciation, an old man with old
hands, standing in the city, the sky *fretted*
with golden fire, pestilence is what he sees,
a beggar and a corpse, and he goes forth,
slipping through the suffering city with nothing
more to want, but the ghost is in the lintel,
and the dead wait with open hands.

tennessee

following williams to mismaloya,
the beach lit up by lightning flashes,
even the iguana cut loose is human,
that was long ago, and just a film
with the usual crew and drunken
actor, but it's williams posing as
an old poet in a wheelchair, isn't
it? his cane falling, his head drooping,
set free, and it's all he wanted,
freedom, even back in the streets
of new orleans, desire's tether
untangled.

yes, she says

oh, the fury of *broken english*, the body's
profane freedom, her hands feeding her
mortal mouth with languages that say almost
nothing, but the hands do, her turning like
a key, or she the small animal crawling into
spirit, and then she stands inside that word,
the brilliant word that touches surrender,
inside molly's word, yes, she says, yes
among the moors and the watchman with his
lantern, women in their shawls and roses,
and a lifetime of furniture, a broken rocking
chair with the graceful old woman in motion
like the stillness of her mind, yes.

a last dignity

ah nina, a spiritual end came, and is coming,
from dusk to dawn, for you in the twenties,
and now as the twenties arrive once more,
for us, with the sun blazing like picasso's light
bulb, click click, berberova on liteiny, reading
a poster of executions, the suddenness of
winter, the way the streetlight is obscured
and newspapers scurry along the sidewalk,
poets meeting in their only clothes and galoshes,
a scent of perfume from one, and fearless
poems in emaciated rooms, some dancing
cheek to cheek, yes a last dignity, these figures
in night's window, and we have come a century
to something like a failure of courage, now.

a young woman in an old dress

a comet across the soviet sky, or a letter
in akhmatova's mailbox, marina has the
chill of the poem in her body, no line
between what is and what is not, love
never small talk in a café, but a scar, and
only the inside matters, weather and
streets, as with all things of the world,
become prayers and the poem arrives
when you have nothing left she says,
when you are spent, when even the
seven bells are silent on the seven hills,
still at the end of their ropes.

marina, marina

it's eros, *take me, I'm yours*, that
longing to enter the other body, to be
wrenched once more out of familiarity
and into the mystery of desire, that
footing, that momentum of existence,
the trail of the poet, her walk through
despair, the arc of the poem, and the
poem, like abramovic's tall body, is
breaking open, is opening its veins,
howling refusal at the mad world,
marina of bruises and marina of
the rope and door.

moriarty

moriarty dazzled in his brown corduroy
jacket and his golden silk shirt, he spoke
lightly, though his laughter went deep,
a voice like this can only be buried in serious
ground, as larkin had it, among flowering
grasses, moriarty chagrined by the rosary
in his pocket, but carrying it nevertheless,
one day a beam of fall light fell through
the high window, a day long ago, I heard
awe in his voice, I heard disbelief, as he
lectured on the sermon on eternity in
a portrait, and I heard how religion can
vanish into something true, these are
not trim gardens, though we are always
at them with our shears.

a kindling glance

a kindling glance, as hardy put it, and almost
anything can happen, though not sainthood,
nothing of airless heights, nothing of account,
there being only a small fire outside the door,
a glance and nothing direct, it is reckless and
at odds with divinity, drowned in gravity, of
the happy grave, if it be such matter, or each
moment's delay of the grave, well, whatever
the name, whatever an end, the theft of a spark,
a breath on it, and a blaze that discomfits the gods.

two stories

two stories, could be dickinson's house,
that soft step on the stairs, an ascerbic
word or two, a way of binding old wounds,
her shoveling snow off the porch, keeping
the walk open for someone who never
arrives, someone she has imagined, some
darwin or chagall, some brilliance behind
a mask, and warkov hunting through magazine
ads for an image, something large enough
to hold her vast memory, and the fissure
running through it, something to fill the bare
almost empty, echoing house.

big sur, or *hello winnipeg*

I call out a greeting to the old man of big sur
and he answers with *hello winnipeg*, well that's
a story to keep with mine, did he skip stones across
the assiniboine? a kind of eternity straddling earth
from long before the bulls of lascaux to long after
the future, comes a time for a skinny-legged kid
to find his way around community clubs and dance
halls, finding his way into the eye of the hurricane,
that long hard way through locations and discoveries
and the shape of spirit, all the way to big sur in a
parking lot at deetjen's, lanky and turning with a grin.

arkin

his hands move in elegant gestures, hands
infused with music and the kindness of
loneliness, arkin in his crisp white shirt and
suit moves through streets and rented rooms
in goodness, the gentle depth of it, the certainty
of it, and his hands, I think, could light a man's
cigarette with a firefly, he could soothe a drunkard
with his supple fingers, their quick precision, those
fine-boned fingers in their wit and nuance, a man
of sadness shaping the music he cannot hear.

oh, by the way

fedora pushed back on his forehead, seeing
the ship off, *bon voyage, have a wonderful*
time, jason robards doesn't *mean maybe*,
he's a thousand clowns opening an act, and
he doesn't know anyone on board, he loves
to stand in the flying confetti, ropes cast off,
bon voyage, another beginning as the ship's
horn sounds, and I didn't care, careless,
carefree, sitting in the garrick theatre, singing
that's my baby, and *oh by the way* that's my
life, a daydream and soon a summer shadow,
remembering now the cracked mirror of my
face, the funhouse, and my birthday in july.

Artists in poems of homage

joe: remembering joe rosenblatt joe rosenblatt
butoh tatsumi hijikata, yukio mishima, and kazuo ohno
among the leaves of light maggie nagle
koestler's window arthur koestler and *boy*, my dog
circus pina bausch
desert harry dean stanton (in *Paris, Texas*) and rainer maria rilke
blood oranges eve joseph
ghost in the lintel marianne nicholson, shakespeare
tennessee tennessee williams
yes, she says margie gillis and james joyce
a last dignity nina berberova and pablo picasso
a young woman in an old dress anna akhmatova and marina tsvetaeva
marina, marina marina tsvetaeva and marina abramovic
moriarty john moriarty and philip larkin
a kindling glance thomas hardy
two stories emily dickinson, charles darwin, marc chagall, and esther warkov
big sur, or *hello winnipeg* neil young
arkin alan arkin (in *The Heart is a Lonely Hunter*)
oh, by the way jason robards jr. (in *A Thousand Clowns*)

Acknowledgements and Notes

Thanks to Eve Joseph and Nathan Dueck for their fine editing.

Thanks, once again, to Marijke Friesen for excellent cover and book design, and to Niko Friesen for musical collaborations.

Thanks to Sue Sorensen at CMU Press, for her thoughtful comments and queries.

Three prose poems were published *in subTerrain* and two in *Prairie Fire.*

The videos *Maria* and *Margaret, Walking* can be viewed under Audio/Visual on the website: patrickfriesen.com.

Welcome Kwúsen to our family.

Remembering Brian Brett, Michael Olito, and Les Brandt.

Afterword: In Hindsight

Over his lifetime in letters, or at least the fifty years since the publication of his first collection of poems in 1976, Patrick Friesen has been open about his suspicions regarding the past. More specifically, he distrusts the epistemology of history—but there's no call for that kind of academic jargon here. With *Sightings*, Friesen doesn't dispute historical facts so much as suggest that their interpretation could use work. And that labour must continue, since a lot of the past remains unknown and there are always alternative versions of that which is known. Friesen puts it this way in "circus": "and I'm born / into the past, not knowing if it's past at all."

An animating tension of the poems collected here is how hard it is to comprehend the past on its own terms. As in "the future, again," identifying a chronology is one thing, but tracing a continuity is something else altogether. That poem opens by questioning a memory of a fruit tree, proceeds to doubt the connection between generations on the same land, and closes by pondering how birth is where death begins. In a way, Friesen observes the womb-tomb poetics that Dylan Thomas developed in "The force that through the green fuse drives the flower," only the former tends to look back where the latter is prone to look forward. Both rhapsodists know better than to draw a line between cause and effect, for there are far too many knots along the way.

Twelve years after his first poetry collection appeared, Friesen contended with his own past in an essay provocatively titled "I Could Have Been Born in Spain." Friesen's thesis was simple: "I was born into this. I could have been born in Spain ... Or Ireland." With the demonstrative pronoun "this" ending the first sentence, he referred to his Mennonite inheritance. Literally speaking, it's impossible for Friesen to make a plausible claim to Spanish heritage, but he knew that readers knew this, so that premise was self-consciously playful. "When I was 11 or 12," he recalled, "I thought I must have been an Irish foundling. I had the name." What's more, Friesen related that when he was a child, his mother often "sang me to sleep with Irish ballads. She named me."

When he grew up, Friesen steeped himself in cultural traditions that spoke to him. Popular music is one such tradition. In his 2006 essay "There Was Always Music," Friesen recollects when "I heard rock and loved it. That energy and release. I still like it, though I tend to return to the musicians of my late teens and early twenties." He names some rock 'n' roll bands that captured his imagination, along with jazz and classical performers, but he remembers falling for "the head-first propulsion of rock." So, not only was young Patrick informed by the ancestral, linguistic, and religious milieu of his community, he was also shaped by practices of his choosing. The ending of his new poem "lies and beauty" hints at the vulnerable moment before he chose to pursue poetry, "before I fell into words, / before lies and beauty and the possible / difference between them." In hindsight, the prose fragments that make up his argument in "I Could Have Been Born in Spain" cast a model for reading the personae he developed through poetry.

Friesen's prose-poem "I Want to Return" presents an elusive presence that's perceptible but not conventionally distinct. The speaker begins with the lyrical address "I want to return, if you don't mind." Then, after describing "an open wound," he uses a pronoun without a specific referent: "It's none of the above, or none of the below." But readers are not to worry too much about such a reference—"Leave that to the birds and fishes." Those creatures, which make up the ecosystem of the air and sea, are uniquely capable of going where the current takes them. Humans, alternately, want to distinguish the beginning from the ending, and we think we need to mark all the points between. Next the speaker observes that "Someone is singing, always singing" to the point where he "Can't get a word in." Those ongoing songs produce sound that's unignorable, but that doesn't mean it's easily grasped. To appreciate the song, the reader needs to accept whatever the senses provide.

In the last section of *Sightings*, "Homages," Friesen presents a series of poems that might fit into the poetic heritage of apostrophe—writing that addresses an absent audience as though it's present and able to hear the message. What's remarkable about some of these poems is how Friesen responds to his influences. "big sur, or *hello winnipeg*," for example, addresses Neil Young, and "the old man" kindly replies. Over a scant twelve lines, Friesen conflates time and space, and the scene takes place upon the rocky shoreline of imagination. The speaker ponders whether the folk rocker took a moment on the road to "skip stones" over the Assiniboine River. He then muses about "a skinny-legged / kid" playing gigs "around community clubs and dance / halls" before eventually "finding his way into the eye of the hurricane." (As Young sings in "Like a Hurricane," that eye is where the calm is.) In the same breath, the speaker teases that he has knowledge he will not share: "well that's / a story to keep with mine." That memory remains a memory, no matter how much readers would like to know it.

In that 1988 essay "I Could Have Been Born in Spain," Friesen reveals that he has always embodied contradictions: "I have been ashamed of my heritage. I have been proud. I have been confused by this heritage. What is it? What was it?" That questioning spirit quickens *Sightings*, to provocative effect. These poems range and return to the past, these lines bend and turn in on themselves, these words warp and turn into others. Friesen is paying homage in many of these poems, but now after a half-century of publishing poetry, he earns and deserves homage himself.

Nathan Dueck

Nathan Dueck is the author of three poetry collections: *king's(mere)*, *he'll*, and *A Very Special Episode*. Raised in Manitoba, he studied at the University of Manitoba and received his doctorate from the University of Calgary. He lives in Cranbrook, BC, where he teaches at College of the Rockies. His latest book is the creative memoir, *(1979-): Mortifications*. For CMU Press, Dueck is the editor of the Lyrik Poetry Series.

Patrick Friesen, born in Manitoba, now lives in Victoria. His first poetry collection, *The Lands I Am*, was published in 1976, and since then Friesen has released nearly twenty books of poetry, including *Flicker and Hawk* (1987), *You Don't Get to Be a Saint* (1992), *Blasphemer's Wheel* (Manitoba Book of the Year, 1994), *The Breath You Take from the Lord* (2002), *jumping in the asylum* (ReLit Award, 2011), and *Outlasting the Weather: Selected and New Poems* (2020). His 1997 collection *A Broken Bowl* was shortlisted for the Governor General's Award, while the play adapted from his book *a short history of crazy bone* won the Winnipeg Theatre Award for Outstanding New Work in 2018.

He is also the author of *Interim: Essays and Mediations* and has often collaborated with musicians and dancers, such as pianist Marilyn Lerner and choreographer Margie Gillis. Several recordings of text and music, including *Buson's Bell* and *Old Man, Shaking His Rattle*, are collaborations with Niko Friesen. He created and produced radio and film productions for Manitoba Education and taught at various colleges and universities, including the University of Victoria.

With Per Brask, he has translated five books of Danish poetry, one of which, *Frayed Opus for Strings & Wind Instruments* by Ulrikka Gernes, was shortlisted for the Griffin Poetry Prize in 2016. His poetry is featured in the bestselling anthology *15 Canadian Poets x 3*, edited by Gary Geddes, while his influential book of poetry *The Shunning* (1980) has been adapted as a radio play, a stage play, and a dance work.